THE ESSENTIAL GUIDE TO POSITIVE
CRATE TRAINING

THE ESSENTIAL GUIDE TO POSITIVE CRATE TRAINING

Crate Training with Kindness: Modern Rewards-Based Methods for Dogs & Puppies

Julie Naismith

pitmore PUBLISHING

ISBN 978-1-9992966-7-4

Cover and interior design: Amanda Baye
Edited by: Jodi Brandon
Cover photo credit: iStock.com/cmannphoto

AUTHOR'S NOTE

Throughout the book I've applied the masculine **him**, **he**, or **his** when referring to both male and female dogs. This in no way reflects a gender bias, but rather is used for simplicity.

RESULTS DISCLAIMER

While every effort has been made to accurately represent how to get your dog over separation anxiety, there is no guarantee that you will. Even though separation anxiety training has a high success rate, there is never any guarantee with behavior change. Any professional who tells you otherwise is not being transparent.

Examples of successful cases in this book are not to be interpreted as a promise of results. Successful resolution is entirely dependent on the person doing the training and on each individual dog's condition.

CONTENTS

INTRODUCTION

Oh, **crates! Other than prong and shock collars, there are** few tools more controversial in dog training circles. Over the years I've been told I come across as pro-crate, anti-crate, crate-obsessed, and crate-hating. Not sure why I'm perceived as having all those (conflicting) positions, but it depends on who you ask, and what they've heard me say or seen me write.

For example, in my Separation Anxiety Heroes membership group, I teach safe crate training. In fact, I include a crate-training plan in the Be Right Back! App that my members use. And I've written about crating without fear in all my books.

I can see why anyone who only saw these resources would think I'm pro-crate.

On the other hand, I'm also a vocal advocate for getting dogs out of crates. I suggest that all my clients, and the members of Separation Anxiety Heroes, do separation anxiety training with their dog out of a crate unless there's a cast iron reason to do so (and even when it seems there might be a reason, I can usually give separation anxiety clients alternatives).

So, I guess this is where the view that I'm anti-crate comes from.

As with many situations in which the court of public opinion has passed judgment, the truth lies somewhere in the middle.

✻ ✻ ✻

In North America—and to an increasing degree the UK—crates are now seen as an essential tool. The advice to crate puppies, convalescing dogs, or dogs who chew seems to be the standard for most dog professionals. North Americans don't question crate use and see it as normal.

However, this widespread use and acceptance in North America hasn't always been the case. It's relatively new.

In fact, the degree of crate use in North America raises eyebrows elsewhere in the world. Some countries don't even permit the use of crates. Many have rules outlawing extended crating or banning the use of a crate that is too small for a dog.

What problems are crates fixing, in countries where they are widely used, that trainers and dog parents elsewhere are struggling with?

The answer: none. Crating doesn't magically resolve problem behaviors. The only functions of a crate that are hard to replicate are travel, transportation, confinement for working dogs, and confinement for dogs immediately post-surgery. Those countries in the world that apply a general ban on crating still permit these specific uses, for the most part.

But everything else that crate-loving nations associate with crating, we can do without a crate: housetraining, preventing chewing, separating dogs, giving dogs a space to cozy in, recovery from injury, and illness.

So why write a guide to crating? Because crating isn't going away. My hunch is that crate use will increase in countries outside of North America, where it's not currently the majority practice (for example, the UK).

And because pet parents will continue to crate dogs, and because crating can be fraught for both dog owner and their dog, I want to guide you as to the kindest, gentlest, and most effective way to use crates as part of the way you care for your dog.

A crate is a tool that has its uses. That's it. I'm anti using crates with anxious dogs, crating dogs for too long (apologies if trainers have told you to do this with your dog), and incorrect advice that crates solve behavioral problems that are driven by emotion.

I'm pro using crates for safety, for crowd control (as we call it in my multi-dog household, where spats are a thing), for travel, and for creating voluntary hidey-holes that dogs can take themselves too.

MY FIRST EXPERIENCE WITH CRATES

The first time I used a crate was when my India was a puppy. I wasn't a trainer then, but I was deeply into dogs. Crating a puppy wasn't something I'd considered, though, until another trainer recommended it.

So, I added a crate to my shopping list and brought home an ugly, rattly, black-wired contraption for my puppy.

She took to it immediately. She's always adored a crate. Yep, one of those dogs.

But although she was little Miss Chill in her crate, I rarely needed to use it with her. She didn't chew, destroy, or have accidents. I housetrained her by taking a week off work and being on high alert for seven days, rewarding her every time she went outside, and not scolding her when she slipped up.

The crate was redundant. I packed it flat and stashed it in a cupboard under the stairs, along with all the other things you buy when you get a puppy, but end up not using.

It wasn't until I followed my passion to become a dog trainer that I heard more and more about crates. It seemed to be the thing—a requirement, not an option, for successful dog parenting, if for nothing else than to housetrain successfully. This seemed especially so with US–based trainers, where I'm not sure I recall seeing any advice other than to crate to housetrain.

The concept is that a puppy would rather hold it than soil in the small, confined space where their bedding also lives. Layered onto this, the crate—or so the advice went—was a puppy's safe space, calming and natural. (More on the concept of safe spaces later in the book.)

So dog parents come home from the pet store with a crate and usually vague instructions on how to use one—just as I did all those years ago.

THE HISTORY OF CRATES

According to a why.org article, the first crates were patented in the 1950s and 1960s. These included the classic wire crate that we so often see today. This was produced by a company whose principal product had been wastebaskets. They brought their wire crate to the market after they'd seen pet owners transforming their wire trash bins into crates.

The article states that the first references to crate training and denning first surfaced in the 1980s and links to a pamphlet with instructions on how to use the crate for dog behavior issues. That pamphlet seems no longer available in the original location, but I did find versions on other sites. Some of the advice in the 40-year-old pamphlet includes this extract:

> *If your dog could talk, this is how he might well express his reaction to using a crate! He would tell you that the crate helps you to satisfy the "DEN INSTINCT" inherited from his den-dwelling ancestors and relatives, and that he is not afraid or frustrated when closed.*

This may not have been the first or only reference to dogs loving crates, to them needing to den, and about dogs not being afraid or frustrated when crated. But this represents the pervading advice that we hear today in the crate-loving countries of the US, Canada, and. to a degree, the UK.

In countries where crate use is less prevalent, this advice is not the norm. In fact, in some places, such as Finland and Sweden, owners can't use crates if their dog is home alone. And in Italy, confinement spaces need to be a minimum of 200 square feet.

Wherever you are in the world, this advice about dogs denning and naturally taking to crates is outdated.

In this book, we look at why dogs needing to den, and seeing the crate as a den, is a myth. We also cover why dogs don't just naturally love crates and why they do, in fact, often become frustrated or frightened when crated.

Let's start with the thorny issue of the denning instinct.

Dogs and the Denning Instinct: Myth or Fact?

The first line of an American Humane Society article on dogs and dens states: "Dogs are den animals." No debate—a statement of fact, it would seem.

In North America, and increasingly in the UK, we have normalized crates, and the defense is that dogs like to den and crates are dens.

But if you asked someone or Sweden, where strict laws govern crating, or in Italy, where, by law, dogs need to have a minimum space of 200 square feet, you'd likely get disagreement with this statement.

I want to unpack that logic, though, because I worry that crates, rather than solving problems, are creating problems, most definitely for dogs and often for humans too.

Are Dogs Really Den Animals?

Let's look at the research and start with wolves.

Dogs are not domesticated wolves, and modern dog training has long since ditched the concept that dogs are just mini wolves. They are not. They are a different species. We shouldn't be basing our care for dogs on badly interpreted notions of what wolves do in the wild. We need to be cautious about assuming that what applies to wolves also applies to dogs.

However, since we so often hear that dogs, just like wolves, love to den, we should examine the research around wolves and dens.

There are a reasonable number of studies into wolves and denning. The overwhelming consensus is that wolves den, but only when they have pups—then and only then. And what's more, it's that only the female who dens.

On top of this, wolves typically have multiple dens from which they choose. Oh, and those dens? They aren't cages. They don't have doors. Wolves and their pups are free to come and go.

What research there is about wild dogs and denning suggests that their use of dens is even briefer than that of wolves.

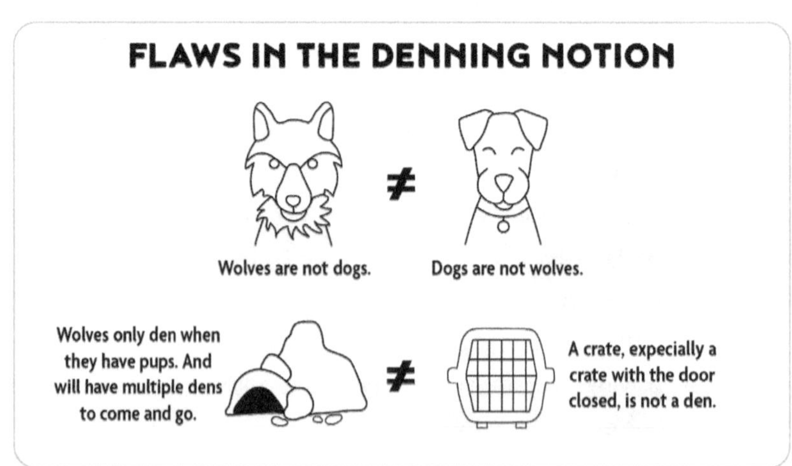

At best, then, we can conclude that female dogs may want to take themselves to a crate when they have a litter; that they would like to have the choice of which artificial dens to use, and to come and go freely (no doors); and that they would abandon their artificial den altogether once the pups are whelped.

It's time to stop saying that dogs like to den and, hence, will love their crates. This is harming to those dogs who:

- Are crated despite hating it.

- Refuse to be crated and are thus seen as problems.

- Accept the crate and end up spending way too long in the crate as a result.

The advice is also unhelpful to pet parents who either don't want to crate their dogs or who think that they must but grapple with a dog who doesn't take to crating.

In this book, we examine when and why you might want to crate your dog. We consider the alternatives if you don't want to use a crate. And we review how to crate train properly, so that your dog chills in his crate should you need to use one.

CHAPTER 1

Crate Myths and Misconceptions

used to be neutral on crates for most situations. I didn't want pet parents to use them for dogs who have confinement or separation anxiety (I strongly advocate against this), but I was neutral about the use at other times.

I was (and still am) pro crates for managing tricky moments with dogs who don't get along or for dogs who don't like people.

The more I researched over the years, though, the more I question whether we really need to be using crates at all. I'd like to challenge the accepted wisdom of the problems that others will say are best solved by crates (especially dog professionals in North America and the UK).

PROBLEMS WE SOLVE WITH CRATES

We know crate use isn't widespread in many countries where dog ownership is. Do those nations have dogs who don't struggle with the same problems, allowing caregivers to dispense with the need for crates?

Not at all. Dog owners in those countries just find other ways to solve the same problems.

Yes, crates can help with certain issues, but they are rarely essential. On top of that, far from solving all dog-parenting issues, crates can exacerbate or cause them.

Here are some issues that result from crating:

- Exacerbated separation or confinement anxiety

- Boredom or even zoochosis (a form of psychosis that develops in captive animals)

- Crate injuries

- Dogs being relinquished because they can't be crate trained

On the other hand, crates can help with the following:

- Preventing damage to our things

- Keeping warring housemates apart or keeping fearful, aggressive dogs away from people, especially kids

- Keeping dogs still and comfortable when they convalesce

- Housetraining

- Safe travel

- For working, sports, or show dogs

From this list, the only three that don't have superior alternatives are handling aggressive dogs, accommodating working or sports dogs, and airline travel.

Finally, let's look at issues that are not solved by crates (despite the claims):

- Separation anxiety

- Home-alone barking

- Anxious house soiling

- Wanting to escape

- Wanting to chew or destroy

Crate manufacturers will tell you that crates absolutely do "fix" separation anxiety, chewing, or escaping.

They absolutely do not fix separation anxiety.

With chewing, destroying, or escaping, if crates seem to prevent these issues, what's happening is the dog's behavior is being suppressed. These behaviors are driven by emotion, namely anxiety. And crates do nothing to change how anxious dogs feel.

Myths and Facts about Crating and Separation Anxiety

My focus is separation anxiety. As such, I come across a widespread, inappropriate use of crating. It's time to bust some of those myths and set the record straight.

Myth

Crating your dog will resolve separation anxiety.

Fact

Crating won't resolve home-alone issues and may make them worse.

We used to think that crating a dog would help home-alone anxiety. Plenty of trainers still say this. But here's the thing: Many dogs who have separation anxiety also have a phobia of crates. For these dogs, crating adds to their panic.

Do we know why crate phobia and separation anxiety seem to go hand in hand? Not really, though if I had to guess, I'd say the crate might add an extra level of isolation for a dog who already feels scared when alone.

Or maybe a dog who has separation anxiety has just spent too many long absences in his crate and associates the crate with scary alone time.

Yet, if you have a dog who's chewing the walls or ripping up the floorboards, a crate can feel like the only answer. It does stop the damage to your house, but you risk severe physical and psychological damage to your dog. Panicking dogs will harm themselves trying to escape. The memory of the panic is lasting.

To an anxious dog, though, a crate is not a haven. It's a punishment.

Myth

Dogs like to den and see the crate as their safe space.

Fact

There's no evidence that dogs like to den, and dogs aren't born seeing a crate as a safe space.

As I covered previously, just because we see wolves denning, we've made the leap that dogs do too, and that the den they would choose is a closed crate. It certainly seems that some dogs like a den-like setup to nap in. And dogs who are frightened of thunder or fireworks may choose to huddle in a crate.

However, even if this is some adapted form of denning, there's a big difference between denning and crating: Dens don't have doors.

Dogs are free to enter and exit dens. With crates, however, we think that by closing dogs into a crate they will feel safer. For many dogs, the opposite is true, especially if we haven't gone through the fear-free crate training plan (and sometimes even if we have).

Thunder-phobic dogs might like to hide in their crate, but they can freak if they aren't free to exit. The same is true of dogs who are frightened of alone time or confinement.

If you want to make a crate into a safe space for when you leave, do it. Just leave the door open and let your dog choose whether he wants to enter and whether he really does feel safe in there.

Myth

If your dog is okay in his crate at night, or when you're around, he'll be okay when you leave.

Fact

Him being okay in his crate at night doesn't mean he'll be okay when you leave.

You might be confused as to why your puppy or dog seems fine in his crate at night, but as soon as you crate him when you try to leave, he loses it. This is a common scenario. For whatever reason, some dogs decide they are okay in their crate in a certain context, but not in another. It makes sense in his head.

If getting him comfortable in his crate at all times is your goal, take comfort from the fact that he's shown he can be okay in his crate in one context. Don't force him to be okay all the time. Help him develop crate confidence in other contexts.

Myth

"Anxiety crates" or indestructible crates are the answer.

Fact

"Anxiety crates" or indestructible crates don't resolve problem behaviors; they suppress them.

You may have seen crates that promise to "fix separation anxiety" because they are constructed such that the dog or puppy cannot escape. These supposedly indestructible crates may be just that—but dogs still injure themselves with escape attempts. And even if there's no physical harm done, the neurochemical damage done by locking a panicking dog in a cell-like crate he hates may be irreversible.

Myth

A crate is essential for housetraining.

Fact

You can housetrain without a crate.

As I explain in the later chapter on housetraining, you can housetrain without using a crate. In countries where crates are rarely used, people housetrain puppies without issue. You just need to take a different approach.

Myth

If you want to prevent destruction, you need to crate your dog or puppy.

Fact

You don't have to crate your puppy to prevent destruction.

You might wonder how on earth you can trust your puppy when you leave if you don't use a crate? First, you can set up a puppy-proofed area (see Chapter 7). Second, if your puppy or dog is chewing or soiling because he's upset, then not leaving him for longer than he can handle will stop this. Third, if you're doing home-alone training (which I cover in other books in the Be Right Back! Series) you'll be watching his every move on camera, so you'll be back way before he gets up to anything.

Myth

Separation anxiety training is best done with your dog in a crate.

Fact

Separation anxiety training is best done with your dog given free rein.

Contrary to outdated advice, separation anxiety training is best done with your puppy or dog out of his crate. You can do separation anxiety training with your dog in a crate, but it's a lot more work.

If crate training just isn't working out for you and you keep getting stuck (Step 13 of the crate-training plan seems to be the biggest stumbling block for most puppies and dogs), then don't do it. It really isn't essential. But if you are determined to get your dog to be happy in his crate when you leave, continue. Just know that it will take more time and require more effort.

As you can see, there are powerful arguments in favor of using a crate and powerful arguments against using a crate. There will be occasions where the decision is out of your hands, and we'll look at those situations in the next chapter.

Chapter Takeaways

- Much advice that you will come about crates and crate training is outdated and unhelpful.

- Understanding what's a myth and what's a fact will help you make the right decision about whether to crate your dog.

- We can easily address plenty of problem behaviors that we used to assume only a crate could resolve.

CHAPTER 2

When Crates are Unavoidable

There will be times in the lives of some dogs when crating will be more a requirement and less of an option. In this section, we look at these different situations.

Flying

Whether you are forced to, or choose to, fly your dog, the airline will require you to use a crate. In Chapter 3, I explain how an airline crate differs from a typical crate. Airlines also have information about the crates you must use.

Whether your dog will fly in the temperature-controlled cargo hold or in the cabin with you will depend on the size of your dog, the airline, the country of departure, the destination country, and the time of year.

Where your dog will fly will affect the crate choices available to you.

Bottom line, though: Even though the makeup might be different, it's still a crate. If your dog hates his crate at home, chances are he'll hate his crate when it's in a cargo hold. Therefore, helping your dog to be comfortable in his crate before flying should be a priority.

Give yourself several months and follow the Crate Training with Kindness Plan set out in Chapter 3 If you have no choice but to fly your dog, then it's vital that you help him feel comfortable when crated, even if he freaks out about it now.

Will your dog love to fly if you get him to love his airline crate? Will he happily chill in his crate for the entire flight if you condition him to be happy in his little plastic box? Some dogs do. Some dogs still hate it, no matter how much work you've put in.

But even though crate conditioning might not be the magic fix for dogs who have to fly, it's a necessary, if not sufficient, requirement.

CASE STUDY

Dog Behavior Consultant Toni Clarke's Journey with Menchie to Comfortable Flying

Flying with a dog can be daunting for both the owner and the pet. However, it's often a necessary endeavor. Despite challenges, there are strategies to ease this process for dogs.

Toni, facing a move to Italy from the U.S., had no alternative but to fly with Menchie, her dog, as driving was impossible and leaving Menchie was not an option.

Preparing for Menchie's first flight, Toni was determined to minimize stress. Long-haul flights are tough for dogs, typically involving travel in a crate in the cargo hold. The journey involves extensive waiting: after check-in, before and after loading, for customs clearance, and finally, for pickup. It's a lengthy ordeal.

Recognizing this, Toni focused on equipping Menchie with the skills to handle various steps and encounters, along with the diverse sights, sounds, and sensations of flying.

Toni's extensive research informed her decisions, considering:

- Optimal airports and routes.

- Ideal travel times, factoring in weather at both departure and arrival destinations to avoid extreme temperatures and potential travel disruptions.

- Choosing airports with fewer delay histories.

- Selecting a crate meeting IATA standards with proper ventilation.

- Opting for a seasoned pet transportation company, especially for international travel.

Meanwhile, Toni started a program to familiarize Menchie with different aspects of flying.

As a fellow graduate of Jean Donaldson's Academy for Dog Trainers, Toni, like me, believes in structured training plans. She developed a flight desensitization and counterconditioning plan for Menchie, encompassing crate acclimatization, exposure to simulated aircraft sound and motion, airport sounds, and motion while in crate.

Key elements of Toni's training plan included:

- Starting with a crate pad in Menchie's bed for two days.

- Combining crate and sound of airplane taking off and landing.

- Mimicking crate movement using a helper to shake the crate gently.

- Mimicking turbulence, in the dark, with sudden, intermittent crate shakes.

- Varying lighting levels during sessions.

- Anticipating high noise levels in the cargo hold and adjusting gradually.

- Driving with Menchie in the crate, with airplane cabin sound played through car speaker, to simulate in-flight conditions.

After two weeks of dedicated training, Menchie was well-prepared for flying, comfortably spending up to three hours in the crate amidst various distractions.

The 8-hour flight itself was a success for Menchie, validating Toni's efforts. While this might seem like a significant undertaking, consistent daily efforts can significantly enhance your dog's comfort during flights. Even if the results aren't as perfect as Toni and Menchie's, any effort toward making your dog more at ease during flying is time and effort well spent.

Managing Dogs Who Don't Get Along

Not all dogs get along with other dogs. And some dogs who don't love other dogs end up living with other dogs. This describes my home. As such, I know it's essential to keep warring dogs apart. Freestanding barriers don't always cut it, and that's where crates come in. Crates not only help create separation between dogs, they also keep dogs safe.

Managing Dogs Who Struggle with Visitors or Kids

Inviting visitors over presents a challenge for many pet parents. For some dogs, visitors are just overwhelmingly exciting. These people-loving dogs get amped up and find themselves unable to show restraint. This might be fine when your visitors are dog people. But it's more challenging when toddlers or frail, older relatives step through the front door.

In such cases, you can teach your dog to do something that's incompatible with bouncing all over your guests, such as nailing a calm sit-stay.

However, some dogs are just too excited to handle that and do better when we take them away from the source of the excitement, especially when we give them an enticing Kong or stinky chew to work on.

If your dog loves his crate, then popping him into a crate in another room away from visitors is a great option. Use the Crate Training with Kindness Plan in Chapter 3.

At the Vet

At some point in his life, there's a chance your dog might need to spend a night or even just a few hours in a vet hospital. In most instances, the vet team will crate your dog in the hospital. There are alternatives you can ask your vet about (see Chapter 7), but getting your dog to be comfortable in his crate won't harm him should he ever have to stay at the vet.

At the Groomer

While some groomers operate a crate-free salon, others require that dogs go into a crate when the groomer isn't working on them. And if your dog is happy in his crate, it's one less thing to worry him during his grooming appointment.

If your dog currently hates being crated, and you need to have him groomed, check with the groomer about whether they crate dogs. If the answer is yes, ask if they could make an exception for your dog (explain why). If they won't make an exception, look for a groomer who won't crate your dog.

If all else fails, then you will need to crate train your dog.

At Daycare

As with vets and groomers, some daycares choose to crate dogs at certain times. This might be when staff are on breaks and there are fewer around to supervise off-leash play. It could also be to encourage quiet time. As with my recommendations above, if your dog hates being crated, either ask for an exception or find a daycare that doesn't crate dogs.

Dog Sports

If you have a sports or show dog, then you know that competition rules often require dogs to be crated when they are not competing. Organizers will rarely allow you to be the exception, even if your dog hates his crate (and plenty of competition dogs do).

Given that there will be times where you have no choice but to crate, or instances where you decide to crate, in Chapter 3 we discuss crate training with kindness.

Chapter Takeaways

- Sometimes the decision to crate your dog is out of your control, even in those countries where crating is not the norm.

- You might also need to crate your dog when you have visitors or if you dog doesn't get along with housemates.

- Given that we don't always have a choice whether to crate, it pays to condition any dog to love a crate.

CHAPTER 3

Crate Training with Kindness

If I haven't yet persuaded you that there are other options besides crating, then this chapter will help you train your puppy or dog to love their crate. We'll cover crate type and choice, placement, as well as explaining the Crate Training with Kindness Plan in depth.

CRATE TYPES

Remember that if you follow the Crate Training with Kindness Plan (which you'll learn later in this chapter), you can get (almost) any dog to love any crate. This is especially so if your dog doesn't have a history of having an aversive experience with a crate.

This means that your goal is not to imprison your dog, so you don't need to worry about indestructible, escape-proof crates. Your dog is going to be comfortable in his crate. This means he will not need a crate that is built with military-grade reinforced steel and locks that a safe-breaker would struggle to crack.

The exception, when such a crate might be appropriate, is when traveling. (More on that to come.)

The main crates you'll come across are:

- Classic wire crates,

- Airline-type travel crates,

- Soft crates,

- Furniture-like crates, and

- Impact crates for car travel.

Let's have a look at the pros and cons of each of these.

Classic Wire Crates

These are the go-to crates for many. They are easy to find, come in a wide range of sizes, and are the cheapest crate option.

Pros

- Price

- Availability

- Size options

- Foldable

- Easy to clean when housetraining accidents happen

- Easy for dog to see out, if you have a dog who wants to keep watch on the world

Cons

- Rattly and noisy

- Might be too open for dogs who need peace and quiet

- Don't look great in your living room (if you're worried about that)

- Some dogs find the tray at the bottom aversive (This needs to be covered with a crate pad.)

Airline-Type Travel Crates

These plastic crates come in two pieces bolted together with a wire door. As with wire crates, they come in a range of sizes.

Pros

- Availability

- Size options

- Easy to clean when housetraining accidents happen

- Obviously, these work for transporting a dog

Cons

- Not as easy to store as wire crates when not in use

- Don't look great in your living room

- Small space for dogs to look out of

- Often more expensive than wire crates

- Ventilation (can be an issue, depending on the exact make and model)

Soft Crates

Soft-sided crates are made of synthetic material framed over metal supports. Some come without the metal and are more like bags.

They are most often associated with small dogs. When a dog is small enough to travel in a cabin of a plane (and the airline allows dogs in the cabin), we can use them as travel crates to be placed under a seat.

Pros

- Lightweight
- Low noise
- Easy to store
- Come in lots of different colors, styles, and shapes

Cons

- Not suitable for cargo transportation
- Not durable (While we're not trying to restrain dogs with crates—since we're going to get them to love being in there—these softer crates can get ripped, especially around the zipper.)

Furniture-Like Crates

If you have crates around your home, you probably don't love the look of them. If that's an issue for you, investigate crates that are built to have more of a furniture aesthetic.

Pros

- Look better than standard crates (if you like the look)
- Sturdy construction/durable

Cons

- Price (They cost multiple times the price of traditional wire crates.)

- Heavy and tricky to move around your home. (If you want the flexibility of having crates in different rooms at different times, these aren't for you.)

- The look (These still look like crates and are typically made from faux wood, so you still might not love the look.)

Impact Crates for Car Travel

Dogs need safety considerations when traveling in a car. Crash-tested harnesses properly attached to safety belts provide protection. Another option is to use a crash-test-rated impact crate.

These crates withstand a certain amount of force should your car be in a collision. If you want to crate your dog when he's in the car rather than having him on a seat, then an impact crate is the way to go. Word of warning: These are not cheap.

Pros

- Safety (If car safety is your priority then a crash-tested crate is the way to go.)

- Durability (They are well-built and long-lasting)

Cons

- Price (These are significantly more expensive than other types of crates.)

COVERING A CRATE

Does covering a crate magically make your dog settle? You might think so since there's plenty of advice to do so. However, it's not that simple. It really depends on the dog, on where they are crated, and on what else might go on around them.

For some dogs, a cover creates calmness. For others, it's a layer of isolation that is just too much for them.

Don't automatically assume that covering a crate is right, or even necessary, for your dog. Instead, test whether putting something over your dog's crate helps or hinders.

Note: If you decide to cover your dog's crate, consider whether a covering might make the crate too hot for your dog. And consider whether a totally opaque cover will work better for your dog than one with some transparency.

You don't need to buy a fancy crate cover. I used old bedsheets. They don't look great, but they are cool and breathable, and on the occasions I cover my dog Tex's crate, a bedsheet doesn't cause him to overheat.

CRATE SIZE

There are many articles and blogs about the perfect size crate for a dog. Much of this information is based around getting a crate that isn't too big. "The smaller the crate, the safer the dog will feel" goes the argument.

But, as we explore throughout this book, crates don't just magically make dogs feel safe.

There are situations in which size matters, but otherwise a crate can't be too big. It *can* be too small. If you're going to enclose your dog in a crate for an extended period, make sure they can stand up and turn around comfortably in there.

I also like to provide different surfaces within the crate: soft or hard, warm or cool. Dogs get little choice in their life. Forcing them to sleep or rest on the same surface is just another restriction of choice and control.

If you have a dog who likes to move around the room when he

sleeps, then you want to give him options within his crate.

That said, I've seen big dogs squeeze themselves into the most ridiculously small crates—but that's their choice. After all, dogs choose to sleep in very odd locations, positions, and spaces.

A dog choosing to snooze in a crate that doesn't quite fit is not the same as forcing a big dog into a small crate. Focus on getting a crate that's big enough.

Airline Requirements

Airlines are very specific about crate sizing. Cargo size is limited and is expensive, so big crates are out. If you're flying your dog, then you need to comply with your airline's requirements. Most airlines follow the IATA Live Animal Guidelines. You can find more information on the IATA guidelines at berightbackthebook.com (the resource site for all my books), but in summary they are as follows.

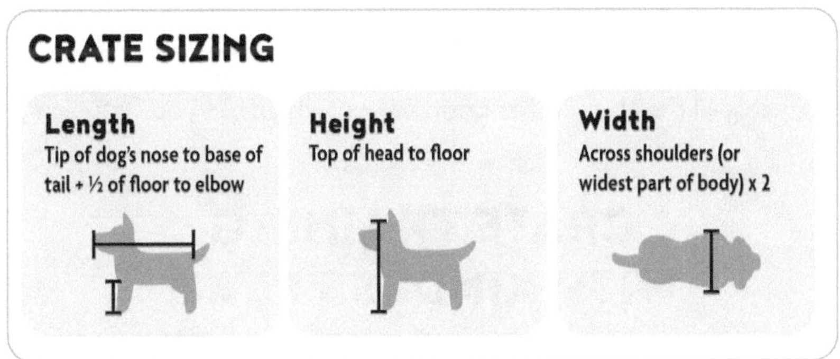

It doesn't matter if your dog hangs out in a crate that's either way too big or way too small (if they choose to do so) at home. However, there are many situations when your dog might have to be crated and the size of crate will be determined by someone else (e.g., the vet, the groomer, an airline). Even with a dog who loves his crate, getting him used to different sizes and formats isn't a bad idea.

Where to Put Your Crate

How do you decide where to put your crate? If you have a large dog and need a sizeable crate, then you may not have many options. Most of us don't have vast rooms in which we can put a 5' x 3' crate wherever we choose.

However, with a smaller crate, or a bigger space, you might wonder where best to locate your dog's crate.

There aren't any rules to this. It depends on you your dog, your home layout, and what you're trying to achieve with crating. Here are some questions to guide you:

1. Are you trying to keep your dog away from noise, away from active parts of the house, or away from windows?

2. Does your dog already have a favorite bed in a favorite spot? If so, consider placing the crate there and placing their bed inside the crate.

3. Does your dog do better when he can see you from the crate, or when he can't see you?

Taking all the above into consideration, where can you fit the crate?

CRATE TRAINING WITH KINDESS PLAN

Now that we've established what type of crate you might choose, it's time to look at the most important aspect of crate training: getting your dog to love his crate.

This simple crate-training plan will help your dog or puppy to love his crate.

While it's true that you can get nearly any dog to love their crate, know that dogs who have had unpleasant experiences in a crate require a lot of time (and a lot of your patience) to warm up to a crate. But it can be done.

My dog Percy used to hate his crate. I'm a light sleeper and he was a bed hog, so I wanted to crate him. He had always hated his crate, so I knew I was in for a long haul. I worked on this plan for six months, training over and over, until he would happily sleep in there at night.

Percy had had unpleasant experiences in his crate when he was a puppy (and when I knew no better). As it is for lots of dogs who've had awful experiences of being crated, progress was slow. They will need a lot of time (and a lot of your patience) to warm up to a crate.

So I know this plan works, and works well. If your dog has hated crate time previously, progress might be slow going for you too.

With Percy, all my hard work went to waste in the end. I missed the snuggles more than I missed my sleep! He's back on the bed and we all love it.

Note: Even though I got him to love his crate, I wouldn't have dreamed of leaving him in a crate if I went out.

I recommend you don't crate your anxious dog when you are out, either. Even if you are diligent, follow this plan to the letter, and have a dog who then adores crate time, know they might still freak out when crated when you leave.

What You Need

- A crate that's an appropriate size for your dog (For more information on choosing a crate, refer to the "Sizing a Crate" section earlier in this chapter.)

- Yummy treats (lots of them!)

- Tons of patience!

Be sure to follow these **"grading" rules:**

- Work in sets of five tries.

- If your dog gets it right four or five times out of five, move to the next step.

- If your dog gets it right three times out of five, repeat the current step.

- If your dog only gets it right one or two times out of five, drop to the previous step.

PHASE I Getting Him Comfortable with Freely Entering the Crate

STEP #	WHAT YOU OR YOUR PUPPY NEED TO DO
1.	Randomly throughout day, drop treats at the back of the crate. • *Keep going for three days until he charges in as soon as he sees you open the crate.*
2.	Use a treat to lure him into the crate, feed at the back (toss treat), let him exit at will. • *Move to step 3 when he does this five times in a row.*
3.	Lure him into the crate and continue the flow of treats (~1 second apart) as long as he stays in the crate. (Still let him exit freely.) • *Move to step 4 when he will stay in the crate happily for one minute.*
4.	Point to the crate to hand-signal him into the crate and continue the flow of treats (~1 second apart) as long as he stays in the crate. (Let him exit at will.) • *Move to step 5 when he will stay in the crate happily for one minute.*
5.	Point to the crate to hand-signal him into the crate and feed and continue the flow of treats (~2 seconds apart) as long as he stays in the crate. (Let him exit at will.) • *Move to step 6 when he will stay in the crate happily for one minute.*

PHASE II   Getting Him Comfortable with You Closing the Door

STEP #	WHAT YOU OR YOUR PUPPY NEED TO DO
6.	Hand-signal him into the crate, move door to half-closed, feed, let him exit.
7.	Hand-signal him into the crate, close door, feed, open door, let him exit.
8.	Hand-signal him into the crate, close door for two seconds, feed, let him exit.
9.	Hand-signal him into the crate, close door for three seconds, feed, let him exit.
10.	Hand-signal him into the crate, close door for five seconds, feed, let him exit.
11.	Hand-signal him into the crate, close door for 10 seconds, feed, let him exit.

PHASE III   Adding Duration

STEP #	WHAT YOU OR YOUR PUPPY NEED TO DO
12.	Make the crate very comfy with bedding, hand-signal him into the crate, give stuffed Kong or other special chew object, close door, hang out next to the crate reading or watching TV for 10 minutes, dropping treats in every 20–30 seconds. • *Do this four to five times over two or more days.* • *Move to step 13 if he goes in without delay and displays no signs of distress when in there.*
13.	Repeat step 12 at a different time but now occasionally get up and leave room. Return within a few seconds. • *Do this four to five times over two or more days.* • *Move to step 14 if he goes in without delay and displays no signs of distress when in there.*
14.	Repeat step 12 at a different time but now for 30 minutes and feeding less frequently (every couple of minutes). • *Do this four to five times over two or more days.* • *From here you can increase duration as long as your puppy displays no signs of distress when in the crate.*

This plan works. It works especially well for dogs who are neutral about their crate or have never been crated. Remember that dogs who have had unpleasant experiences in a crate require a lot of time (and a lot of your patience) to warm up to a crate.

1. Be ready to "split" (aka work on a step slightly harder than your current one, but slightly easier than your next one). For example, perhaps you find your dog aces step 10 ("Hand-signal into the crate, close door for 5 seconds, feed, let him exit"), but struggles with the next step where the duration is now 10 seconds. And you find this happens more than once. In which case a good split would be to have a 7 or 8 second duration.

2. Take as long as you need at each step. This applies to all dogs, but especially to dogs who are starting from a point of hating their crate. Step 13 is often the hardest for many dogs, as it's the transition point to you being out of sight.

3. Try a new crate. This can help dogs who have had a bad experience in a crate in the past. For example, if your dog was left in an airline crate and developed a fear of crating, try a hard-sided, airline-style crate. Sometimes even just a new crate will help the training. If you have other crates in your house, try training with a different one.

If you follow this plan, try all three tips, and your dog still isn't loving his crate, then at some point you need to decide to call it quits.

Once your dog gets truly comfortable in their crate, you may notice that they take themselves off to their crate even when you don't ask them to.

You might also find that, if they fall asleep in there when the crate door is closed, that they don't immediately spring out when you open it.

You can tell a dog who truly loves cozying in his crate when he gives you that "can't be bothered to move" look when you first open the door.

Lots of dogs are so driven to be part of the action and so curious that they can be in the deepest of sleep in there and still ping to life as soon as you touch the catch, so this isn't a definitive test of whether your dog loves his crate. But you can be sure that a dog who barely raises an eyebrow when they hear that crate door clink is extremely happy in his space.

Our goal is to have a dog who is so happy in his crate that the closing of the door is incidental. Now, you might say, if the goal is to have a dog who loves his crate so much, we barely need the door, then why bother crating at all? Why not just use "go to your place"?

To me, it's like recall training. I want my dogs to be so good at recall that I don't need a long-line to keep them safe. But I might still choose to put a long-line on my dogs, as an extra layer of security. It's not the long-line that teaches them to come when called. It's the recall training.

And it's not the closed crate door that teaches a dog to be comfortable in their crate, it's the crate training.

As I said earlier, we can get nearly any dog to love a crate...but we can't get all dogs to love a crate.

There are better dog-training plans to put your effort into than banging your head against a crate wall. If a crate matters to you, and you're just not getting there, other options for confinement and management that don't involve crates, then I cover all this in Chapter 6.

How Long Should You Crate Your Dog?

If you've gotten this far, hopefully you've met your goal of being able to get your dog to love his crate. You might be ready to put his new crate-loving into real-life action.

Maybe you want to use the crate when friends with kids come around, and your dog doesn't love having toddlers in his face. Or maybe you are considering crating your dog when you go to work (provided your dog doesn't have separation anxiety, of course).

Here's the thing, though: When you succeed, and have a dog who loves his crate, who goes in there willingly, and who doesn't break down the door when closed in, as soon as you clunk the crate catch over, your dog no longer has choice.

Dogs don't get a lot of choice as it is, but you've decided that crating your dog for several hours a day works for you. It most likely doesn't work as well for your dog, however much he loves being in his crate.

You know that feeling you get when you've been on a flight too long? You're stuck, you can't change where you're sitting, and you feel cooped up. Well, imagine your dog having to put up with that every day.

It's tolerable. It doesn't make us anxious. But it's not how we'd choose to spend our lives. And at least on a plane we can choose to get up for a stroll and we can choose which movie to watch. We have some choices.

Leave your dog for several hours and what choice does your dog have? *Shall I lie at this end or that end? Shall I turn around or stay put?*

I'm not trying to bash you. Somewhere along the way, you've likely read or been told by a trainer that dogs can be left in a crate for extended periods of time. This advice isn't incorrect; dogs *can* be crated for long periods of time. That doesn't mean they *should* be crated for long periods of time.

What trainers omit when they give you this advice is that this should be the rare exception, not the norm.

I'm fascinated that with zoo animals, best practice is to reduce the number of animals in captivity, because we understand the detrimental impact captivity has.

For those animals who remain captive, zoos have changed their husbandry models intending to make enclosures and cages bigger, and reducing the time that animals spend in small, confined spaces.

Yet, the internet, and lots of trainers, must think that dogs are wired differently than ever other species in the animal kingdom. Why else would they suggest dogs can benefit from eight hours in a crate? When did you last hear the narrator of a natural history documentary say, "The lion was moved to a tiny cage in order to reduce his stress by making his world smaller"?

Dog trainers tell us that making the dog's world smaller is a good thing, especially for an amped-up dog.

I'm sorry if a trainer or other professional has given you this advice. It's not fair to you or your dog that people give such unqualified advice.

Crating your dog for long periods of time, day after day, isn't good for your dog. And it's unnecessary. There are plenty of alternative solutions for whatever problem you're trying to fix with a crate.

CONFINEMENT, CRATING AND LEARNED HELPLESSNESS

You might have heard people say they never had to train their dog to be okay in their crate. They might add that their dog made a fuss or cried initially, but that they made their dog tough it out.

These owners might scoff at your gentle attempts to get your dog to be okay in his crate.

So how did they do it? How did they get their crying dog to be okay in a crate?

Maybe a dog who initially freaked out in a crate, but then accepted crating, is in fact displaying what we call learned helplessness.

Learned Helplessness

Learned helplessness is a condition that can develop in any subject who has little control over a situation it finds aversive.

It doesn't matter what I do, this thing keeps happening to me. So I'm just going to stop offering any behavior, a dog might say.

When a dog stops seeing the connections between their behaviors and consequences, that's when learned helplessness can develop.

If you've ever heard someone say their dog eventually got used to their crate, learned helplessness might be why. The dog might have discovered that escape from a crate was futile and given up.

Here's how that learned helplessness could develop with a crated dog:

- The dog hates the crate.

- He cries to be let out, but that doesn't work.

- He cries for longer and cries louder, but that still doesn't work.

- He now adds howling, and he still doesn't get released from his crate.

Finally, he mixes in scratching, clawing, and pawing. But it doesn't matter what happens, he can't stop the thing that's scaring him: confinement.

Nothing the dog does changes the situation. His attempts are futile, and he feels helpless. He gives up.

Learned helplessness occurs when a dog decides that offering a behavior is pointless, since the scary stimulus doesn't go away, no matter what he does.

When a dog stops offering a behavior, it can look like he is suddenly being "good." Really, he is shut down. He has given up.

The dog hasn't changed the way he feels about the crate. He still hates the crate, but he has no hope of being able to change anything.

But if a dog develops learned helplessness, why would he ever go back into his crate? Because learned helplessness alters the underlying motivation, too. The dog knows he's going to be crated again, and he just surrenders to it.

Whenever we expose a dog to the maximum intensity of something he fears, we are using a technique called flooding. Flooding, as a training process for dogs, is cruel and unethical.

For excellent examples of dogs showing learned helplessness being described as "good dogs", watch any YouTube video of a trainer, such as Cesar Millan, or videos of so-called balanced trainers on TikTok.

They parade dogs in these videos as dogs who they have miraculously transformed. It's true they transformed these dogs—into dogs without hope, with broken spirits, but who are still full of fear.

So don't buy into the "my dog just got over it his crate and now loves it," spin.

Some dogs do, but they didn't hate the crate to start with. They might have found being crated different or new, and hence seemed slightly unsettled. These dogs do quickly habituate.

Dogs who are scared when crated don't just get over being in a crate, unless we cause them to respond with learned helplessness. And that's not the same as them being happy to be crated.

Crate Whining

You might think, "But my dog only whines a little when I crate him, and then he's fine."

It's true that some dogs seem to be perfectly fine in their crate, but start off with some crate whining. Perhaps they whine for a minute the first couple of times they are crated. Then, from that point, they are fine and never whine again.

It would seem they weren't finding the crate aversive. It could be, therefore, that the whining was "I'd rather not be in here" as opposed to "I'm so scared in here."

How can you tell the difference? You can't. Experienced trainers can't always tell. However, if you use the Crate Training with Kindness Plan, you'll be helping the dog or puppy who just doesn't want to be in there, not just the dog or puppy who fears the crate.

Chapter Takeaways

- If you decide to crate your dog, consider several factors, including crate type, placement, and how long your dog will spend in his crate.

- Despite the popular myth, crates aren't natural for dogs. You mustn't just crate your dog and hope for the best.

- You can, however, get your dog to love his crate using the Crate Training with Kindness Plan in this chapter.

- While this plan works for some dogs, a portion of dogs will just never be comfortable in a crate. If this is your dog, you're not failing if you can't train him to love his crate.

Resources

- Crate Training with Kindness Plan
- IATA Guidelines

berightbackthebook.com

Housetraining With or Without a Crate

Whether you have a puppy, a newly adopted dog, or a dog who seems to have regressed with housetraining, you're going to need a plan.

A crucial component of successful housetraining is limiting the access that dogs and puppies have to spaces in the home.

Housetraining only succeeds if you prevent your puppy or dog from having accidents. In the US in particular, crates are used to manage access and prevent accidents. Dogs and puppies hate soiling their sleeping area, and so the smaller we make the area they have, the less likely the dog is to soil—hence, crating.

But a crate isn't the only way to prevent puppies and dogs from having accidents while housetraining. The three other options are:

1. Confining your dog or puppy to an exercise pen
    (sometimes also known as an X-pen) or behind a baby gate,

2. Tethering your dog to you, using a leash attached
    to your waist if you can't watch him every minute
    or simply carry him around with you, and

3. Dividing rooms into small spaces in which you hang
    out with your dog (dual confinement, I guess!).

The last option is the approach I took with my own dogs. I housetrained all my puppies without a crate, and it pretty was easy. I used gates and barriers to contain them in a smaller space *with me* rather than have them in a space separate from me.

Once you've decided how you're going to limit access, it's time to get training. For the housetraining plan, you need:

- A schedule for going outside,

- Treats for when you go outside with your puppy,

- Good observing skills to prevent accidents, and

- Patience.

Step 1: Determine a Schedule

Provide your dog with a set schedule for eating and for going outside. A typical puppy housetraining outing schedule looks like this:

- First thing in the morning

- Whenever your puppy wakes from a nap

- After each meal (This is often when puppies
  will have a bowel movement. You will
  discover your own dog's rhythm.)

- After every play session

- Depending on the puppy's age, every 30 to 90 minutes

For a dog who's going through a housetraining regression, you can use a similar schedule to begin with. A dog should be able to hold it much longer than a young puppy, but there's no harm in taking your dog out frequently when you first start on remedial housetraining.

Step 2: Take Your Puppy or Dog Out According to the Schedule

Once you've determined your schedule, take him outside to toilet.

Use the same spot each time, so he associates the area with its purpose. Don't interact with your puppy. Just let him get on with it.

If nothing happens after five minutes, bring him back into the house and contain him for 30 minutes. Then try again.

If he does eliminate outside, give him a supervised free period in the kitchen or confinement area, or—better yet—an enjoyable walk. This acts as a bonus for "performing."

A very young puppy (six to eight weeks) may need to go out once during the night.

Step 3: Reward Generously

Every time your puppy eliminates outside, heap on the praise and produce a favorite treat. If the praise makes him stop in the middle of eliminating, save it until just after he finishes. Have treats and his leash near the door, so you always have them ready.

Step 4: Hone Your Observation Skills

Puppies give signals prior to eliminating. If you learn your puppy's signals, you'll catch far more would-be accidents before they happen. Common signal behaviors include circling, restlessness, and sniffing. Whenever you see these, take the puppy out!

Step 5: Don't Lose Your Cool

Most puppies will have accidents, especially at the beginning of training. Since your puppy will only be free to roam in the kitchen when he is "empty," mistakes will be seldom.

If your adult dog has had a housetraining setback, be patient with him too. You might also want to see the vet in case there is a medical reason for your adult dog's housetraining regression.

Step 6: Supervise and Repeat

Supervise so you can take him out if you see him winding up. If you see him starting to eliminate, say, "Outside" in a bright, gentle tone, and get your puppy or dog there as quickly as possible. Don't shout at your dog! Never punish, as this may inhibit your dog from going in front of you. Punishment doesn't have to be physical. It could be a sharp word.

Stay outside for the five-minute period, and praise and give a treat if he finishes. If he doesn't go, bring him back inside and either supervise or crate him for another try later.

If your puppy or dog has an accident in the house or in the crate and you did not see it happen, do not punish him. It won't work and it's cruel. Clean up the spot and apply a commercial odor neutralizer. Vow to supervise more closely in the future and/or add another trip outside to your schedule.

HOUSETRAINING NOTES

- If you are following the schedule and your puppy or dog is still urinating several times per hour, take your puppy to the vet.

- With a puppy four months or older and still having accidents, my guess would be that he has too much unsupervised, loose time in the house. Remember that each time he goes in the house, he is being de-trained and is learning that inside is the place to go.

- If your goal is for your puppy to go outside, paper training is unnecessary. It might seem like more work initially to always have your puppy pee or poop outside, especially if you live in an apartment block in Canada and your puppy wants to go out at 10 p.m. on a January night! In the long run, though, it's less work to train without paper. Train him to go on paper first and you're just putting off the inevitable work of having to train him to go outside.

- If your adult dog was previously housetrained but has regressed, you can still use this same plan.

Chapter Takeaways

- Housetraining without a crate is just as effective as doing so with a crate.

- You will need to be more diligent, and you still need to consider how to limit your dog or puppy's space. But you can ditch the crate.

- Housetraining well relies on you monitoring your dog or puppy, rewarding consistently, and never punishing accidents.

CHAPTER 5

Nightime Crating

A popular use for crating, even with dog parents who wouldn't otherwise crate, is to have puppies or dogs sleep in a crate overnight.

It's common for dogs to be okay in their crate at night, and then hate their crate at other times. There is no rational explanation for this, other than your dog has decided what's safe and dangerous. That's all.

However, if your puppy is having housetraining issues at night, or if he has zoomies at 1 a.m., or if you've decided you want him in your room but not on your bed, then you might have decided to crate at nighttime.

Why Dogs Like to Sleep on Our Beds?

Given the choice, most dogs would prefer to sleep on a bed with their human. You may have read or heard that when a dog sleeps on your bed, he's asserting his dominance or leadership over you. This isn't true.

There's no evidence that dogs are in any way trying to be our "leader." The alpha myth has long been debunked.

The reason dogs like to sleep on our beds is that beds are comfortable. Dogs are social sleepers, so a comfy spot where everyone is sleeping is the natural spot for dogs to head at bedtime.

What to Do if You Need Your Dog to Sleep Elsewhere

Dogs can develop anxiety at nighttime, even if they've been downstairs peacefully snoozing on their own for years. Perhaps they're now wandering upstairs. Or maybe you're closing doors, only to find you're woken by scratching in the middle of the night.

If so, you might be tempted to assume the answer is to crate. However, if your dog has become anxious overnight, crating him won't help.

Here's what to do instead.

If your dog's issue is you being out of sight at night, you want to teach your dog that he can handle being at home with you in another part of the house. You might need to do this even if your dog doesn't struggle with separation anxiety at other times of the day.

Use the Magic Mat training and do it in the spot you are going to designate as your dog's sleep zone. Start by working on Magic Mat during the day. (See "The Magic Mat Game" in the Appendix.)

Gradually increase the time you are out of sight. Your goal is to be able to go upstairs and spend 30 minutes in your bedroom while your dog stays wherever you want him to sleep. Whenever your dog comes to find you, gently take him back to the mat. It's important that you do this consistently. He needs to learn that he's okay on his own on the mat and that following you upstairs doesn't mean he gets to stay upstairs.

You can do Magic Mat training using his bed if that works better. And as you increase the time, you can relax the criteria from "stays on mat/bed" to "stays downstairs/out of the bedroom."

Repeat the steps in the Magic Mat training, but do so in the evening.

Then do Magic Mat training at bedtime. To make this as easy for you as possible, I recommend heading to bed an hour earlier. This might be hard, given your busy schedule. But far better to do this training and still have your full complement of sleep than be sleep-deprived.

Don't jump from one hour out of sight in the evening to a full night. Start with one hour per night. Then extend that to two.

Be Consistent

Once you know your dog can sleep on his own elsewhere—because he's demonstrated as much with the foundational out-of-sight training you did—now is the time to be consistent. If he cries, don't ignore him. Go to him, but do not let him come into the room.

It's critical that if your dog wakes up, you don't let him scream, whine, or cry it out. Equally, if he does vocalize, don't automatically let him onto your bed. Go to him, but—just as you do with children who wake in the night—resettle him there rather than bringing him into your room. When you first start this process, you can resettle him by sitting next to his bed. On subsequent occasions, gradually move away. You might settle him while sitting on a chair next to his bed, then sitting on a chair further away from him, and then standing.

You might well experience the night of the 100 walks (or several nights of them!), but you do need to do this every time. Go to him, resettle him, go back to your bed, and repeat, repeat, repeat.

Nighttime training isn't easy. In the short term, you're going to have some sleep deprivation and disrupted nights, but if you're consistent and hold your ground, you can teach your dog to sleep in his own space. If your dog will just not accept nighttime crating, you might give up and let him sleep on your bed. If so, just know that having your dog sleep on your bed won't cause behavioral issues.

Chapter Takeaways

- Nighttime crating is popular with lots of pet parents.

- If your dog is okay in his crate during the day, but hates his crate at night, try not to stress. This is more common than you might realize.

- With patience, consistency (and some initial loss of sleep for the humans) most dogs can learn to sleep through the night in their crates. If you decide it's easier all around to have him sleep on your bed, you're not doing anything wrong and will not ruin your dog.

CHAPTER 6

Confinement

Perhaps you've tried the Crate Training with Kindness Plan, but it's just not working for your dog, despite all the tips I shared. If this is you, please don't feel defeated. Some dogs never take to a crate, and your dog may be one of these.

But what do you do if you absolutely must contain your dog?

One option that works for some dogs who just can't be okay in a crate is a confinement area. A confinement area gives your dog more space than a crate, and some dogs are okay with this setup, even when they can't handle being crated.

Plenty of dogs hate crates and hate confinement too, but if you have the right equipment, this approach could be worth a try. (Later in this chapter we cover equipment options for confinement and space management.)

When deciding where to confine your dog, consider:

- How much does it matter if your dog can hear or see outside from his confinement space?

- If you have options, would you rather put the confinement space on a carpet or your hard flooring?

- How high does the confinement space need to be for your dog? Will your dog be able to jump over it?

- Does partial confinement work, as in using a barrier such as an exercise pen combined with furniture or used to block off a corner of a room? Or does a freestanding area make more sense?

- What will you put in the space? At the very least, you'll want to leave your dog's water bowl and something comfy for him to settle on. (If he destroys his bed, you've probably already gotten him a bed he can't decimate.)

- Will you put the confinement space somewhere that allows your dog to hear and see you easily? Or is popping him out of sight better for your dog?

- If you have other dogs, will they also be in the space? Will they be in their own space? Or will they be given free rein?

There are no rights or wrongs here. The answers to these questions will be very dog-dependent. Learn what works for your dog, and just answer the questions based on whether it makes it easier or harder for your dog to be confined.

CONFINEMENT TRAINING

If your dog doesn't immediately take to being confined in an exercise pen or behind a baby gate, then you can use a training plan to get him gently accustomed to being separated from you.

You can use Magic Mat training. (See the Appendix.) Put his mat (or special bed) inside the confinement space. Where the Magic Mat plan mentions *room*, think *confinement space*. For *door*, think *door to the pen* or *baby gate*.

Baby Gates and Barriers

Baby gates can be a handy way to set up a confinement space. These gates also help to manage open-plan spaces. Open-plan spaces are great for living and are increasingly popular. They are awful for dog management, though!

Perhaps you have dogs who need to be separated from each other, such as a stiff, sore senior who needs a break from the new, in-your-face puppy in the house.

Or maybe you have parts of your home that you want to prevent your dog accessing. You might have decided that you need to protect your things. (See Chapter 7 for information on how to do this.) In any of these situations, open-plan living is a challenge.

Luckily, parents (human parents, that is) are often similarly challenged with open-plan living—for example, parents who don't want their toddler slipping out of the living room into the kitchen, when Mom or Dad turn their back for a second.

And because human parents face the same logistical headaches, there are plenty of products, designed for human babies originally, that fit the bill for sectioning off areas in the home. These are typically long, concertina-like, freestanding barriers, with a built-in gate.

I love the freestanding options, because they don't need to be fixed to a wall, can easily be moved around to wherever needed, and come in lengths that work in most homes.

The longer ones aren't especially high, though, so if you have a dog who leaps barriers, these may not work.

Exercise pens are the dog version of long, extendable baby gates, with some key differences though in that they:

- Aren't freestanding when extended.

- Need to be in a pen formation to stand without being attached.

- Usually aren't as long, so in a big room, you'd need to use more than one.

- Are typically made of wire mesh rather than the simple bars of the baby gate.

While exercise pens come in greater height options than extendable baby gates, if you do go for height, you sacrifice stability.

Extended exercise pens work best when deployed in combination with the strategic placement of a large piece of furniture. The lack of stability makes them less useful than extendable baby gates, if you're trying to portion off a large space. But when you combine them with sturdy furniture, they become more robust.

Exercise pens and extendable baby gates are fabulous for fencing off your furniture, kitchen, or anything else you're trying to protect.

A final option is freestanding dog gates. These are a handy addition to the space-management toolbox. These are shorter than extendable baby gates but often taller. Most come with legs that can be attached for greater stability.

If looks matter to you, freestanding dog gates are often more attractive than exercise pens. Typically, they aren't long enough to form an enclosure. As with the exercise pens, I've found they work best when used between sturdy pieces of furniture, or in combination with other gates or pens.

Chapter Takeaways

- If you followed the Crate Training with Kindness Plan, and your dog still isn't comfortable in his crate, don't lose hope. You can use other strategies for containing your dog.

- The options for confining your dog include exercise pens, baby gates, and freestanding dog gates.

- You can help your dog be comfortable in their confinement space by using the Magic Mat training covered in the Appendix.

CHAPTER 7

Going Crate-Free

Crates aren't the only answer, but it can seem that for many issues, crates are the only solution. By now, though, you hopefully have learned that in those countries in the world where dog parents don't use crates, people still manage to housetrain, chew train, keep dogs still after surgery, and stop amped-up dogs from causing havoc with visitors.

In this chapter, we look at the crate-free training alternatives available to you. Our focus is on three of the biggest, seemingly required uses for crates, each of which, in fact, you can achieve without crating:

- To protect your things and your dog

- To help a dog recover from surgery or an injury

- When you've been told your dog needs an "off" switch

Let's consider each of those in turn.

To Protect Your Things and Your Dog

To decide an alternative setup for chewing and destroying, a vital first step is to consider why a dog is showing that behavior in the first place.

If they chew and destroy because they're ...

bored

- **Increase the amount of exercise** if he seems to destroy less when he's tired from a great doggie workout.

- **Change the type of exercise**. Maybe your dog needs to sniff more. Perhaps he needs to play more. Work out what your dog loves to do and do more of it.

anxious

- First, work out **what's causing the anxiety**: Is it separation anxiety? Is it noise phobia? Generalized anxiety?

- Once you've worked out why your dog is anxious, **work on the source of the anxiety**. This is the key to stopping this form of destruction.

You need to decide if your dog is having fun or if he's stressed.

If you have a young, curious, high-energy dog, it could well be that he is entertaining himself. Have you noticed that he gets into stuff when you're around, and not just when you're out? If so, chances are he is just enjoying himself.

Another telltale sign can be *what* he gets into. Does he scavenge in garbage cans and take his chances with counter-surfing? Does he get stuck into things that are enjoyable to chomp on, like the heels of leather shoes, the corners of cushions, and the spines of paperback books? Dogs who seek objects like these are often looking to have a good chew just to pass the time.

If instead, though, he is ripping up entrance-way carpets, shredding doorframes, and clawing at plasterboard by the front door, then chances are the behavior is anxiety-fueled, and you address that differently.

If you have a dog who's just having fun, get good at putting everything away—and I mean *everything*. If your dog loves to chomp on shoes, keep shoes in a closet—always. If your dog likes to counter-surf, leave nothing in temptation's way.

This means you must keep your counter free of anything your dog could steal. I know that sounds frustrating. After all, it's a lot of work and easy to forget. Plus, why must you, rather than your dog, do the accommodating? Why can't your dog learn?

While he can learn not to counter-surf, trying to reason with him to stop stealing cheese is like asking a toddler not to open cupboards. There's a reason we use child locks on kitchen cabinets: because it's easier than teaching an 18-month-old not to investigate a door that looks ever-so-interesting.

If your dog is destroying out of fear, then you change the behavior by stopping the fear. Dogs who harm themselves when crated are also fueled by fear. (I cover fear of being left more in-depth in my books in the Be Right Back! Series.)

Maybe your experience, though, is that your dog doesn't injure himself in the same way when crated. However, if he's a dog with anxiety, it's important to ensure that he hasn't descended into learned helplessness in his crate. (See Chapter 2 for information on learned helplessness.)

If he has just given up trying to escape (rather than stopped wanting to escape), he might not be causing himself any physical harm, but he might well be causing mental and emotional harm.

With these dogs, once you work to change the fear, or stop the fear by not leaving or confining your dog, the fear-driven behaviors go away.

CASE STUDY

Rethinking Puppy Confinement– Patty's Approach with Skippy

The common notion is that crating a puppy is essential for their safety and to protect the home. It's true, a home is a playground of temptations for a puppy, and those tiny teeth can wreak havoc on household items!

However, many puppies find confinement challenging. Using a crate, playpen, or exercise pen often feels like a struggle—and who wants to be in constant conflict with their adorable pup?

It's a daunting task to puppy-proof an entire room. Even with diligent effort, we can still end up wondering, "Have I missed anything they can get into?"

This is where Patty's strategy with her puppy, Skippy, offers a fresh perspective. Patty realized her objectives were twofold: 1. Ensure Skippy's safety, and 2. Protect her belongings. While Skippy's safety was paramount, Patty understandably wanted to preserve her possessions, too.

Patty's innovative approach involved reversing the concept of confinement. Instead of crating Skippy, she fenced in her valuables and potential hazards. The idea is akin to garden protection strategies - like using deer fencing for young trees or wire covers for vegetable patches.

You'll find images of Skippy's 'safe room' and the protected areas on our resource page. Patty cleverly repurposed Skippy's x-pen, traditionally used for confinement, as a barrier to shield her belongings and risky items. It was a stroke of genius!

Patty's solution is highly recommendable. Skippy didn't feel restricted, yet she was completely safe, and Patty's belongings were secure. This approach promotes a harmonious living environment, aligning with the safety and well-being of both the puppy and the household.

To Help a Dog Recover from Surgery or an Injury

I've worked with many owners who are filled with dread when the vet utters the words *crate rest*.

For many dogs, crate rest isn't an issue. They love to be in the crate and are so laid back about being crated that spending hours in there every day during convalescence is tolerable.

However, if you've tried crate rest with a dog who doesn't fall into this profile, you can appreciate the challenge.

Even if your dog is now okay in a crate (because you've done the work and followed the Crate Training with Kindness Plan), extended crate rest could still be a big ask.

Of course, you want to make sure you follow the guidelines from the vet, and you don't want to risk, for example, stitches coming undone or back injuries worsening, so you want to stick to the rules.

It's important to remember, though, what the goal of crate rest is: for your dog to rest. The crate is the means to enable that rest.

If a crate makes your dog panic, he will not rest. If extended time in a crate makes your dog fidget, he is not resting.

That's why you need to remind yourself of what your goal is and how you can achieve this if crate rest isn't working. Here are my two favorite alternatives:

1. Have your dog in a bed next to wherever you're sitting, with them tethered to you. When you move to another spot, move your dog with you. If your dog is large, sitting on the floor next to him will help. If your dog is smaller, you can pop him on the sofa next to you.

2. Be in a small confinement space *with* your dog. Provided that your dog doesn't try to run and jump around the space, you might be able to remove the tether. Be sensible about removing the tether, though.

When You've Been Told Your Dog Needs an "Off" Switch

Pet parents who find that crating works for their dog often say that it gives their dog an "off" switch. It's almost as if, for some dogs, being asked to go to their crate is a trigger that the fun and excitement have ended and it's time to chill.

In fact, this works so well for some dogs, it really does seem like they have an "off" switch that is flicked when they crate-up.

However, for a dog who hates his crate, his "off" switch won't work in the crate. In fact, he'll get more agitated and amped up, not less.

That doesn't mean you can't still teach your dog to settle. Remember that a crate is only a tool, and it's not the only tool. You could consider teaching your dog mat relaxation. (The Magic Mat training I cover in the Appendix does exactly this: It rewards dogs for settling and for settling away from you.) Or if you're using a **confinement** space setup, that could be the trigger to your dog that it's time to chill out.

In countries where crates are not the norm, trainers and owners successfully help dogs to settle without crates—even wired, amped-up, high-energy dogs.

So no, you don't *need* a crate to teach your dog to settle.

PUSHING BACK ON CRATING ADVICE

If you are now convinced and can see that, often, crating can be optional, you might need to convince a skeptical other half. You might also need to push back gently against crate training advice from a dismissive trainer.

If so, here are some scripts to help you win the argument.

Objection

"He'll chew and destroy if you leave him out."

Response

"I can totally understand why you'd crate your dog if you're worried about your dog shredding your carpets and taking chunks out of your wooden dining table.

"And I can see that probably seems like the only option is to crate. We have other options, though. I'm going to (*insert your option here*), and I'm following a plan to make this work."

Objection

"Your dog will get into something he shouldn't if you don't use a crate."

Response

"I know that traditional advice is that crating a dog is the way to stop them getting into things. However, I've learned that it's far easier on everyone if we just put things away. It takes a bit of practice for this to become a habit. But now, if he doesn't get into something, we just scold ourselves for leaving things out, rather than scolding him for getting into stuff. He's just being a dog, after all."

Objection

"He'll harm himself if you don't crate him."

Response

"I know it might seem obvious that, if he's ripping his nails or getting splinters in his gums, we have no choice but to crate him to protect him from further harm.

"But dogs hurt themselves in so-called indestructible crates that can cause serious injuries. And the panic that drives him to escape is terrible for his fearful brain, too."

✳ ✳ ✳

As you can see, there is nearly always an alternative to crating. So, if your dog is still hating his crate even after you try the Crate Training with Kindness Plan, there are other of other tactics you can use.

Chapter Takeaways

- Even when it seems like crating is the only answer to a behavior issue, you may still have options.

- We can learn much about going crate-free from those countries in the world in which crates are not widely used.

- If others aren't on board with you going crate-free, use the scripts in this chapter to persuade them.

The Magic Mat Game

The Magic Mat Game will teach your dog that it's way more rewarding to stay on his mat than to do other behaviors.

You will need:

- A mat that you'll only use for this training (and will put away when not training),

- Lots of great treats,

- The training plan outlined later in this section, and

- The demo video (see www.berightbackthebook.com).

"Grading" Rules:

- Work in sets of five tries.

- If your puppy gets it right four or five times out of five, move to the next step.

- If your puppy gets it right three times out of five, repeat the current step.

- If your puppy gets it right one or two times out of five, drop to the previous step.

- Always reward your puppy in a down position. If he gets up when you're reaching for treats he just earned, get him back into a down before giving him the treat.

The more you practice this, the more magic the mat will become. When you take out the mat, your puppy will rush to it. This is because all that reward training you've been doing has made him associate the mat with treats!

Once this behavior is solid, you can take the mat on the road, which is great for trips to the vet, for visiting friends, or even for eating out (in places where that's allowed).

Here's the plan:

STEP #	WHAT YOUR PUPPY NEEDS TO DO TO EARN TREATS
1.	Hold a down for 1 second with a treat ~2 feet away from the dog at his nose level.
2.	Hold a down for 3 seconds with a treat ~2 feet away from the dog at his nose level.
3.	Hold a down for 1 second with a treat 2–3 feet away on the ground. (If he moves, cover or grab the treat so he can't pick it up.)
4.	Hold a down for 3 seconds with a treat 2–3 feet away on the ground.
5.	(Stand on the other side of your puppy.) Hold a down for 1 second with a treat 2–3 feet away on the ground.

STEP #	WHAT YOUR PUPPY NEEDS TO DO TO EARN TREATS
6.	(Stand on the other side of your puppy.) Hold a down for 3 seconds with a treat 2–3 feet away on the ground.
7.	Hold a down while you take 1 step to the side and back.
8.	Hold a down while you take 2 steps to the side and back.
9.	Hold a down while you take 3 steps around your puppy and back.
10.	Hold a down while you walk halfway around your puppy and back.
11.	Hold a down while you walk a full circle around your puppy.
12.	Repeat steps 7–11 in the other direction.
13.	Hold a down while you walk 6 feet across the room and return immediately.
14.	Hold a down while you step to the doorway and return immediately.
15.	Hold a down while you step out of the room into the hallway and return immediately.
16.	Hold a down while you step out of the room, close the door, and return immediately.
17.	Hold a down while you go into an adjoining room and return immediately.
18.	Hold a down while you go into an adjoining room, close the door, and return immediately.
19.	Hold a down while you step to the doorway and return immediately.
20.	Hold a down while you step out of the room into the hallway and return immediately.
21.	Hold a down while you step out of the room into the hallway, into another room, and return immediately.
22.	Hold a down while you step out of the room into the hallway, into another room, count to 10, then return.
23.	Hold a down while you step out of the room into the hallway, into another room, count to 20, then return.

From here, continue to build duration in another room. If you have stairs, you could add in going up the stairs. You might want to break it down into a few stairs at a time. Or you could use the Magic Mat game to have a shower in peace. And many of my clients bring out the Magic Mat when they take their dog to a dog-friendly pub or patio. There are so many brilliant uses for the Magic Mat game.

Resources

- The Magic Mat Game

berightbackthebook.com

INDEX

T

V

W

Z

Julie Naismith helps owners and dogs around the world overcome separation anxiety and get their life back on track. While most dog professionals work across a range of cases, Julie is one of the few who focuses on a niche.

Julie's specialist knowledge means that she's come across hundreds of different separation anxiety cases and fully appreciates the nuances of this complex behavioral condition.

Not only does Julie help thousands of dogs and their families, her global SA Pro Certification program trains trainers in her method so that, they too, can help dogs overcome separation anxiety.

Julie acquired her skills and knowledge at the Academy for Dog Trainers, often referred to as the Harvard for dog trainers, where she was taught by world-renowned trainer Jean Donaldson.

Originally from Yorkshire, England, Julie currently lives in the Canadian Rockies with her husband and three dogs.

For more information on Julie's programs for owners or for trainers visit: julienaismith.com

www.ingramcontent.com/pod-product-compliance
Lightning Source LLC
Chambersburg PA
CBHW021340060726
47591CB00006B/2109